KEYS ON HOW TO HEAL FROM BAD PARENTING

Ultimate guide on how to heal from bad parenting

O. G. RICHARD

Table of content

CHAPTER ONE

Simply put, emotional abuse is any language or behavior intended to harm a person's sense of self-worth, self-image, self-confidence, or mental health.

Several frequent instances of emotional abuse are provided below:

abusive language (name-calling, yelling, insulting someone)

Rejection and neglect (dismissing and not tending to needs, thoughts, or opinions)

Gaslighting (psychological manipulation used against individuals to make their sense of reality seem invalid)

isolated strategies (control over a person to the extent that they cannot have or build a social circle outside of the emotionally abusive relationship)

Any combination of the aforementioned instances, as well as others, can constitute emotional abuse. It is significant to remember that some may be trickier and more covert, and others may be blatant and clear.

Every decision we make might seem momentous at times, and every error seems important. Particularly when it comes to adverse relationships with our children, we are concerned about the long-term implications of our decisions.
We worry about whether we were too harsh when we yelled at them earlier, if we could have handled that tantrum better, or if we gave the right consequences.

But every parent experiences those times when they lose their composure. We've all made less-than-stellar parenting decisions when we were angry or confused.

There are four main parenting style, according to many psychologists. Each parenting method has a unique approach to raising children, and it will have a different impact on the children. Low self-esteem, behavioral issues, or inadequate social skills are more prevalent outcomes of specific parenting philosophies.
With the help of this knowledge, you may build stronger and more rewarding relationships with your kids if you are doing it yourself

PARENTING STYLES

According to clinical and developmental psychologist Diana Baumrind, parenting styles and children's conduct are directly related. There are four basic categories of parenting, each having distinct traits and a different impact on a child's development. The four categories—authoritarian, permissive, uninvolved, and authoritative—were discovered to be a highly accurate indication of children's wellbeing as well as a forerunner of future achievement, happiness, and stability.

Everything from academic success to physical health to self-esteem has been linked to parenting approaches. Adults who were raised by parents who used a positive parenting approach frequently have a more stable attachment style, greater social skills, and a lower risk of mental illness

AUTHORITARIAN PARENTING STYLE

Authoritarian parents are different from authoritative parents in that they don't care about their kids' feelings or opinions. The following beliefs are typically held by these parents, who are sometimes referred to as "strict,"

Children ought to be seen, not heard.
Children should follow my instructions because I say so, and they shouldn't have too much fun.
These parents demand complete submission from their kids because they think kids should be subordinate. They could impose limits that are extremely tight.
or unreasonable regulations, and any transgressions will result in severe penalties. With little tolerance for humor or fun, this parenting style frequently adopts a no-nonsense attitude.

Despite the best of intentions on the part of authoritarian parents, research reveals that this parenting approach has many negative effects on kids. Children of autocrats typically have a negative outlook on life and are more prone to clinical depression and anxiety. Since they were prevented from claiming independence as children, they may have weak coping mechanisms and remain obedient in adulthood.

PERMISSIVE PARENTING STYLE

People who adopt a permissive parenting style are more likely to act more like friends than as parents. They don't use much (or any) structure ,behavioral issues without sufficient attention, or discipline. Permissive parents risk losing their children's respect since they consistently act leniently rather than as an authority figure.

The likelihood that a child would have behavioral issues and generally have little respect for authority figures increases if their parents are permissive or indulgent. Permissive parents do not sufficiently restrict their children's intake of junk food and candies, which puts them at a higher risk of developing health issues like diabetes or obesity. Due to the parent's failure to instill positive routines and habits, the child is also more likely to have dental cavities or poor oral health.

UNINVOLVED PARENTING STYLE

A detached or inattentive parent doesn't give the child's needs enough (or any) attention. Although it is most frequently a failure to meet emotional requirements or to be a reliable presence, this can go as far as failing to provide food or clothing. They also play a minimal role in their children's day-to-day activities and are unlikely to assist with homework or lend a hand with extracurricular activities. Uninvolved parents frequently don't know where their kids are or who their friends or teachers are. Children of uncaring or uninvolved parents frequently have to raise themselves.

For a variety of reasons, including a demanding career, financial strains, mental health conditions, or substance addiction disorders, parents may be absent from their children's lives. Children of absent parents frequently battle with low self-esteem, and they are more likely to join a bad crowd, attempt drugs, or become parents while still in their adolescent years. They frequently have trouble finding stable jobs as adults, wholesome relationships, or financial security.

As it creates a balance between showing compassion and enforcing the law, the authoritative parenting approach is the most beneficial to use. Parents that are authoritative make a lot of effort to have a good relationship with their kids while enforcing rules and regulations. They are careful to acknowledge their children's emotions and respect their viewpoints. By rewarding good behavior and putting in place reward mechanisms, the authoritative parent engages in positive discipline.

According to research, adult children with strong parents are more likely to be successful, joyful, responsible, and well-adjusted.

Even if you don't have children of your own, this knowledge can be very illuminating for individuals who are attempting to put their own upbringing into perspective.

CHAPTER TWO

How can poor parenting manifest itself?

There are several things that are universally regarded as "poor" by all people.

The most serious and harmful behavior qualities that most of us associate with poor parenting are physical abuse, neglect, emotional abuse, and sexual abuse. These are issues that need to be dealt with right away by experts.

In addition to child abuse and neglect, however, there are other actions or words that parents may employ that may harm a kid—even unknowingly. You might feel better about your parenting if you can identify whether you're engaging in those behaviors.

Poor parenting is when parents don't give their kids enough emotional, psychological, intellectual, or physical support.

It can be challenging to honestly evaluate your parenting approach.
It's not appropriate to label oneself or another as a "poor parent" because of a difference in parenting philosophy. The distinction between having a terrible day and being a bad parent must also be understood.

Losing your temper occasionally is not the same as telling your child that they are stupid or that you are right and they are wrong and there is nothing they can do about it.

Despite the fact that some people disagree about what constitutes "excellent" or "poor" parenting, the majority of parents exhibit both positive and negative parenting traits.

When nothing seems to be going your way and your tolerance is at its absolute limit, it's simple to feel like you are failing as a parent.
However, it's a positive indication that you're not a poor parent if you're worried about whether you're raising your children in the proper way.

In addition, we offer advice on how to focus on the good aspects of parenting because, while we're in the thick of it, it's so simple to focus on the bad.

Which behaviors indicate poor parenting?

When you think about the extremes, it's simple to identify less than ideal parenting practices.

Extra or minimal involvement

On one extreme, you have the neglectful, disengaged parent who doesn't care about their child's needs beyond the bare necessities of food, housing, and clothing.

An overly involved parent (also known as a helicopter parent) can also do more harm than good by controlling decisions and doing too much for their child, preventing them from learning through experience. This is not as harmful as a neglectful style of parenting.

Low or absent discipline

Children who receive little to no discipline are left to fend for themselves, according to Sharron Frederick, LCSW, a psychotherapist at Clarity Health Solutions. This can lead to injuries and also produce children who are unable to understand boundaries.

Children look to parents to define boundaries and the repercussions that can happen if the child crosses them, according to the expert.

rigorous discipline that is strict
Frederick claims that in contrast to parents who enforce little to no discipline, parents who practice strict or rigid discipline (also known as

authoritarian parenting) prevent their child from exploring the outside world, which frequently results in a child who becomes fearful, anxious, or rebellious.

Withholding love and attention

Frederick claims that ignoring a child is like telling them that your love is conditional. Similar harm results when affection is withheld from a youngster because they disobey instructions.

These kinds of actions, according to the expert, "may lead to a youngster having low self-esteem and low confidence, which can lead a child to not express their wants and needs."

Shaming

Children who are routinely embarrassed, whether in public or privately, may have issues with perfectionism and a need for perfection, worry about failing. Depression or anxiety may result from this.

Why are kids not well-parented?

Substance abuse may be the cause of poor parenting.

Since drug addicts frequently think more about how they can ensure their substance supply than how to take care of their children, they may no longer be able to adequately care for you if your parents are addicted to legal substances like alcohol or illegal narcotics.

Therefore, if your parents use drugs while you are a child, you could experience severe neglect.

unwelcomed child

Having children makes some parents very joyful. However, some parents are not ready for it, and as a result, their kids end up being more of an accident.

The majority of the time, these 'unwanted' kids
be treated that well because their parents may not be able to care for them because they weren't supposed to be adopted.

Furthermore, because they are unprepared and do not understand what is crucial, these parents can also be unable to raise their kids in a manner that is right.

Egoism

Some parents are also highly egotistical, caring far more about their own well-being and personal development than they do about their children's mental and physical wellbeing.

If you grow up in such a home, there's a good possibility you could experience severe neglect and other mental health problems since you could not feel like you matter to anyone.

If egoism in parents results in extreme levels of narcissistic behavior, the situation is made by even worse.

Behavioral issues

It's possible that parents who have mental health problems can't properly care for their kids.

For instance, if your parents experience hallucinations or schizophrenia, it's likely that they won't be able to manage their own lives and that you will have to take care of yourself as a child from a young age.

Parents' mental health concerns could also affect their children's physical health if they abuse their kids as a result.

ailments of the body

Physical limitations may also prevent parents from providing their kids with the necessary care.

For instance, if your parents use a wheelchair to get around, they won't be able to cook for you or go shopping when you're a kid.

Additionally, they might not be able to transport you to school, and they might find it difficult to carry out a number of other everyday chores due to their handicap.

As a result, it's possible that your parents can't adequately care for you.
You as a youngster might even need to provide for them.

Poverty
The lack of money may be another factor in poor parenting.
It's likely that your parents won't be able to provide you with a good education or other things that could increase your chances of succeeding in life if you grow up in a household where poverty is a major concern.

Your parents' severe levels of pessimism and frustration brought on by poverty may also raise the likelihood of child abuse or other unfavorable outcomes for your children.

Unemployment

Another aspect of poor parenting may be unemployment.
Your family may experience substantial levels of poverty if your parents are unemployed, which could hinder you from receiving a quality education, especially if you reside in a developing nation with a bad economy.

Your parents' mental health problems brought on by unemployment may likewise raise the likelihood of you raising your children poorly.

Additionally, because children often take after their parents and could behave in a similar way as adults, your chances of being unemployed when you grow up increase.

Overtaxing

The enormous amount of work that children often require can also leave parents feeling pretty overwhelmed.
Because of this, some parents might not be able to handle all of these problems and might not be willing to put in all of this effort.

This could result in neglect and a number of other problems for the aforementioned kids.

A career goal

Even in many workplaces that profess to encourage employees' personal lives, it can be challenging to balance a family with a demanding career.
Due to the fact that both parents would likely work long hours and may not be able to adequately care for their children,

children in families with demanding jobs for both parents may suffer as a result.

Parental Ignorance

The parenting style has a big impact on how educated the kids are as well.

In comparison to children from families where their parents do not place as much value on their children's education, children from parents who are eager to provide their children with educational resources and assist them with their homework are more likely to be able to achieve better grades and attend better schools and colleges. Parenting styles will be impacted if the parent chooses not to share their solid parenting expertise with the kids.

CHAPTER THREE

What effects do bad parenting have on adult children?

Neglect
mental illness
difficulties at school
low educational attainment

financial difficulties
Unreliability
drug abuse
Unemployment
Homelessness
Pessimistic worldview

Neglect

Neglecting children severely can result from poor parenting.

Children are likely to feel completely unimportant if their parents do not value them highly and do not wish to spend enough time with them.

Furthermore, there is a potential that these kids would experience major extra issues as a result of neglect if their parents do not support them with key duties like homework and other responsibilities that kids have.

Mental disorder

Children may experience major mental disorders as a result of poor parenting.
Since they haven't yet established a strong moral foundation, children are particularly susceptible to abuse, neglect, and other negative effects of poor parenting.
These kids may go on to experience mental health problems like depression as a result, especially if they experience additional difficulties in school or other areas of their daily lives. They may feel quite lost in life as a result of their parents' lack of support.

difficulties at school

Serious problems in school may also result from poor upbringing.
For instance, children who experience bullying at school might not receive the

support and guidance they need from their parents to stand up for themselves and end up suffering for a considerable amount of time.

Furthermore, academic issues might also contribute to issues at school.

Children who experience inadequate parenting are more likely to struggle academically and may not be able to enroll in college, which could result in limited job options.

Low levels of education can result from poor parenting, which can affect grades as well as other aspects of a person's life.

This might prevent kids from learning how to fix items around the house or how to go on and handle particular challenges that arise in everyday life.

Since young kids may frequently feel disoriented and ill-equipped to handle situations on their own as adults, failing to teach them could have major consequences.

financial Challenge

Financial Challenges can result from poor parenting, which can affect both parents and their kids.

For instance, the likelihood is that you will imitate their conduct as an adult and behave similarly if you grow up in a home where your parents frequently experience financial difficulties.

Studies have shown that parents have a significant impact on children.

The same is true of financial subjects.

Making matters worse, parents with money issues won't be able to teach their kids how to behave responsibly with their money, and their kids might not learn it otherwise.

Unreliability

Children who are never taught to be trustworthy by their parents may struggle greatly as adults to behave in a trustworthy manner.

However, their lack of dependability could result in a number of problems, including fewer favorable employment possibilities.

Usage of drugs

Another problem with poor parenting is that it makes it more likely that their kids will take drugs.

Children who feel unimportant and neglected may spend a significant portion of their childhood spending time with friends rather than their parents.

If these buddies use drugs, there's a good likelihood that additional kids will feel pressured to do the same by their peers.

This could therefore result in drug dependence from a young age, making it difficult for those kids to quit using drugs.

Unemployment

Children may also experience increased odds of receiving poor work possibilitics and unemployment as a result of poor parenting and the resultant lack of education.

In turn, a number of additional problems, such frustration and drug abuse, can result from unemployment.

Homelessness

In extreme circumstances, poor parenting may also cause a child to become homeless at some point in the future.

People who lose their jobs may no longer be able to afford their rent and become homeless, living on the streets.

This is especially true in nations with either no social security or social security that is insufficient.

When someone in those nations loses their job, it can be very easy for them to become homeless and suffer the negative effects

Pessimistic worldview

Due to their terrible childhood memories, children who have experienced parental neglect or abuse tend to have a more pessimistic outlook on life.
A negative outlook on life, however, is the root of many other problems, including issues with mental health.
Therefore, poor parenting could result in serious problems for these kids later in life, not just when they're young.

This might imply that educational institutions offer after-school programs where kids can work on their

assignments under the supervision of a teacher or tutor.
Additionally, it could also refer to emotional support.

Children should have a place in school where they can go if they are mistreated or encounter other problems because of poor parenting.

By providing children with these possibilities, they may receive the necessary support, and the issues resulting from poor parenting may to some extent be reduced.

Decision-makers in businesses should reconsider the company values in a direction where family and work are more compatible if both parents work hard jobs with lengthy hours.
This could entail setting up childcare centers inside the business so that

parents can look after their kids during lunch or in between meetings.

The overall quality of parenting will probably increase by making family and work more compatible.

These businesses will also likely improve their appeal to highly qualified candidates, which could offer them an edge in the competition for top personnel.,
residential facilities for children

It may be fair to protect these kids by removing them from their parents and raising them in foster homes in very extreme situations where parents are completely incapable of caring for their kids due to drug misuse or other problems.

To ensure that the children in these foster families receive enough levels of care and high-quality care, however, is necessary for their healthy development.

It may be beneficial to offer parents psychological support if they experience mental health problems.

This would not only enhance the general quality of life of the parents, but it may also enhance the parenting of the kids since parents with mental illnesses may not be the best parents.
since parents who suffer from mental illness may be better able to care for their children if they receive appropriate care and assistance.

Parents of children who live in extreme poverty should also receive financial assistance so they can buy them school supplies and other necessities that will give them a fair opportunity at a bright future.

This might also take the shape of educational vouchers, ensuring that parents don't spend the money on drugs or alcohol instead and that it is used to support youngsters from challenging home situations.

There should be enough detoxification facilities available for parents who are drug addicts so that parents who are ready to stop abusing drugs can receive assistance in completing this challenging task.

This is true not only for parents, but also for kids who are already drug addicts.

Additionally, there have to be initiatives that work to stop people from using drugs for the first time, as doing so may help stop people from developing addictions in the future.

Self-reflection

It takes sincere self-reflection to succeed in all aspects of life.

Everyone has limitations and flaws, but it's important to be aware of them.
You can only begin to combat your weaknesses in a constructive way if you are aware of them.

The same is true of poor parenting.
You can only gradually raise the standard of parenting if you constantly evaluate your actions and ask yourself what you can do to do better.

Self-development

This is a subject that is closely tied to self-reflection.

Once you've recognized your flaws, attempting to correct them is essential to raising your parenting game overall.
This should also involve asking other parents how they handle particular issues so you may gain a more comprehensive understanding of the subject and incorporate practical advice into your parenting approach.

It is essential to raise the general level of education in order to combat the problem of bad parenting.
People may be better able to see their own flaws and work on them in order to improve themselves and their parenting style if overall education is improved.
Assistance to neighboring kids
You should encourage other children in your area who appear to be facing major issues at home in addition to doing your best for your own kids.

Try to assist these kids if you recognize them.
This could mean talking to their parents since many parents may not even be aware of the many problems their children may actually have to deal with.
It could also mean telling their school about their issues.
In today's society, bad parenting is a major issue.

Many parents neglect to care and nurture their children properly because they are simply too preoccupied with their own issues.

As a result, it is imperative that organizations like schools or other facilities take action to support kids from challenging family situations.

Only then would it be feasible to eventually raise the standard of

parenting for many kids around the world.
What consequences result from poor parenting?

Without supportive parenting, kids are more likely to experience problems in their personal relationships, as well as aggression, despair, and anxiety.

The consequences of persistently bad conduct patterns are listed below. There is a difference between that one incident when you yelled at your child for shattering your beloved coffee mug and a practice of persistent criticism or physical abuse.

The excessive use of negative labelling and shaming is a parenting mistake that can have long-lasting effects.

Consistently using derogatory terms, such as calling someone names, negatively affects a child's sense of self and causes them to develop negative self-narratives and self-fulfilling prophecies over time

This is a strong, paralyzing feeling that permanently alters one's identity and sense of self. Due to its power, Dorfman claims that many people—including parents—create it in order to discourage bad behavior or inspire good behavior.

Dorfman asserts that when shame and derogatory labels are used frequently, kids start internalizing and acting out these messages.

They begin to speak to themselves in ways that reinforce their bad emotions and make them severely critical of themselves, she says.

People who have low self-esteem tend to look for partnerships that will support the messages they have been exposed to.

According to Frederick, children who are subjected to too rigorous or rigid discipline may have problems with controlling others, obsessive-compulsive disorder, and other worrisome tendencies, along with the belief that the world is hazardous.

The rebellious youngster, on the other extreme of the scale, argues with their parents, disobeys the law, and behaves badly.

behavioral and emotional issues

Children who experience harsh parenting, which involves verbal or physical threats, repeated yelling, striking, and quick negative consequences for a particular action, may develop emotional and behavioral problems.

CHAPTER FOUR

How to Heal From Narcissistic and Emotionally Abusive Parents

You'll discover suggestions for healing from childhood trauma below. Please take note that this part is predicated on the reader realizing they are the adult children of abusive parents and that they wish to end the cycle of abuse.

Accept and acknowledge the truth

Recognizing emotional abuse for what it is is the first step towards healing. Many victims, especially if the abuse wasn't physical, aren't even aware that it's happening to them. It can be difficult to comprehend emotional and psychological abuse since it can be so subtle and covert. If you want to heal, acceptance is essential. Stop wishing you had devoted parents. Stop attempting to transform a person with a personality disorder into a caring person. It will never occur. Recognize that one or both of your parents is unable to love you and treat you like a person rather than a possession. Such a heartless monster won't be interested in your happiness, only in what you can do for them or how you can help them.

Forgive

Some victims are unable or unwilling to comply with this. Personally, I believe it to be an important move. You need to forgive yourself, not the abuser. It's about not letting your abuser occupy as much of your thoughts and feelings, about being able to let go and go on. It doesn't imply that you should forget what was done to you. Additionally, it does not entail explaining it away or allowing the abuser to believe that the horrible treatment they perpetrated on you was acceptable.

You don't need to address the perpetrator or even hint at your forgiveness to them in any manner. You can compose a letter to them and either shred it or preserve it in your notebook. There may be a "open"on your blog without mentioning them by name. The important thing to remember is that it's a healing practice. And if you discover that you are unable to forgive your abuser, forgive yourself at the very least. Yes, a lot of survivors experience unjustified emotions of shame and guilt.

The majority of the time, abuse victims blame themselves for a variety of features and behaviors that the abuser has put onto them. If your abusive parent had a bad day, they probably blamed it on you. As a result, it's only natural that you've learned to accept responsibility for things that are not your fault. Do you routinely apologize to someone even when you've already

A person who experienced abusive parenting as a youngster will understand the lasting effects that it would have on him. To heal, it will take a lot of time and work, but it is doable, and every little bit helps.

Realize that you weren't at fault

It is not your responsibility, therefore do not hold yourself accountable. Because we are expected to "respect" our parents as their children, society often frowns upon persons who criticize them. We're expected to put up with anything they do to us. And because they "gave us life," we are also obliged to respect and adore them without condition.

It's possible that you turned your parent's cruel actions towards you into self-blame in an effort to make sense of it. Because to the outside world, if there's a problem with your connection with your parents, there must also be a problem with you. But things don't work like that.

Your parent did you wrong. And on occasion, being close to them makes you a more attractive target.

And consider this: No matter how you acted or how challenging your parent's life was, it does not excuse their treatment of you. They were the adult; you were the child.

I'm sure all your parent's verbal abuse, manipulation, and scapegoating did a number on you. If they were depressed, stressed, or whatever else, it is their responsibility to deal with it or find healthy ways to cope, NOT take it out on a helpless child. And you probably still apply the same punishment to yourself now.

It's challenging to undo early programming that has been ingrained in you. But make an effort to understand that your parents' critiques and allegations of you are entirely the result of their own unresolved issues, not yours. Narcissists think they are never at fault for anything. Before they even consider blaming themselves, they will accuse the entire world. So it stands to reason that your narcissistic parent will accuse you of being the problem because "What's wrong with you? Your parents care about you.

Every time they experience insecurity, disappointment, or failure, narcissists criticize others. They undermine you in order to elevate themselves. Extreme rage, drama, and attempts to project superiority are more likely to occur when someone feels insecure. Because of this, they attack you.

A narcissist will criticize you in an effort to make you feel inadequate, unimportant, and wounded. It instructs you to keep your head down and aim low. It's their method of keeping you under control so they can feel in charge.

It is not your responsibility because your abusive parent was the main cause of the abuse you experienced, not you. Don't hold it against yourself if your parents are unable to love, respect, and empathize with you.

Recognize that they probably learnt how to behave from their parents. There are several generations of abusive parents. When there are multiple generations involved, it becomes less personal. (More to come on this.)
Your parents did not mistreat or fail to love you because of you. You weren't chosen for it; you were born into it. Before you arrived, the abusive habits were already in full force.

as a child, you were pure. Nothing you did could have improved their love for you or their treatment of you. You'll never really understand why they are unable to, though. But keep in mind that it is unrelated to you.

Once you acknowledge that nothing was your fault and that no matter who you are or how you behave, it wouldn't have changed how your parent treated you, you can begin to recover.

Discover the effects of the abuse on you.

You need to understand how the abuse affected you and contributed to who you are today in order to be able to truly heal.

Identity is Shaped by Experience.

You likely had many erroneous notions ingrained in you by the abusive parent, which you took to be true. It's possible that you are unaware of how these beliefs affect how you see the world and yourself. They remain undetected, affecting you without your knowledge.

Unconsciously, you dictate to yourself what you can do, think, feel, have, how much of it, and how frequently. These unconsciously held ideas ultimately determine who you choose as partners, how much success you are permitted to

have, and the caliber of your relationships and emotional health.
You were given a defective set of messages that make you more likely to act against your own best interests. Your defense mechanisms against maltreatment as a child may have developed into self-destructive habits.

The driving force behind how you act, think, and feel is your endeavor and battle to obtain the acceptance, love, respect, and affection of others since you were deprived of it as a child. You were deceived into thinking that your worth and lovability are determined by your deeds, appcarance, and/or accomplishments.
No matter how successful you are or how loved and cared for you are, these bad behaviors and feelings continue throughout adulthood. In a way, it's as if you're looking for specific circumstances

to reenact comparable ones in an effort to find a happier resolution to the losses and disappointments you experienced as a youngster.

You must first recognize the issues you're facing in order to heal and stop your negative thoughts, emotions, and actions.

What do you now want to modify or improve? Maybe it's your lack of self-assurance, negative habits, or despair.

After determining the issues, research the situation and make an effort to comprehend it cognitively. Try to ask these questions to yourself:

How does the issue manifest in symptoms and behavioural patterns?

How does it impact my life?

*Where did it come from?

It's time to confront your old problems and deal with them once you begin to understand how the past has affected the present. And in order to do that, you must modify how you see yourself and your life as well as process your history.

Analyze the past

The hardest part of healing can be dealing with the past. You can experience the sensation of reliving your prior maltreatment. But there's no need to relive it; just make an effort to reflect on and recall it.

Investigating every facet of yourself is necessary for recovery. It entails determining what aspect of your

personality is a result of the trauma you experienced.
You will probably experience a lot of rage or despair as you go through this process. You can be upset with them or even with yourself for allowing them to treat you badly. You might experience regret or melancholy for not receiving the parental and childhood affection you deserved.

Although going through this procedure will hurt, it allows you to express your emotions. If you don't deal with your internal grief or anger, it will always be a part of you and cause you harm.

You must accept the reality of your own suffering. Even while it might not seem like it, holding it within and repressing it only makes you feel worse.
Be in mourning for the child you who was denied life because of your parents. Be in

mourning for the parent you did not have and will not have.

Being upset or unhappy that you didn't get the love you wanted and deserved from a parent is acceptable and even beneficial. Work with the emotions rather than ignoring them.

Consider what just happened and how you felt at the time. Avoid making excuses for your suffering, such as "I shouldn't feel this way" or "I don't have it that bad." Try to avoid allowing other individuals to do the same. It is useless. Instead, start letting go of whatever it is that you need to let go of, and keep going until you start to experience relief.

Because you've spent your entire life being trained to repress your feelings, it could be challenging. You might think it's strange or uncomfortable to pay oneself emotional attention. But you are not longer required to act as though everything is alright when it is not.

In order to prevent yourself from becoming an abuser like your parent, it's important to be able to stay with challenging emotions and pay attention to what they're trying to teach you. Also keep in mind that this doesn't have to occur all at once. Repeat it as often as necessary until you feel better.

Writing as a Healing Tool

Writing is a technique that many experts advise using in this process.

You can create poetry to communicate your ideas and feelings, keep a journal to process your childhood experiences, or engage in a letter-writing exercise to explore the foundations of your connection with your parents.

Find out more about the therapeutic power of writing, as well as some journaling prompts and a letter-writing activity, in this post: Healing from Childhood Abuse through Writing

Accept the world as it is

Accepting your past, your experiences, your suffering, your abusive parent, and yourself is esscntial to moving on. Because "if onlys" are all just wishful thinking that keep you mired in fantasy, you can't stay stuck in them.

You have to stop telling yourself, "If only I was a better child," or "If only they had better parents," in order to be able to

accept the fact that your parents were violent and unloving. You must accept the situation as it is.
Avoid concentrating on the "why," as you might never discover the answer. You'll never fully understand your parents' motivations for acting in certain ways toward you.

Healing comes from looking at what happened, how it affected you, and what you can do about it now.

Recognize that you cannot go back in time and change what happened. Recognize that you cannot change the way you felt in the past or how it influenced who you are today. And acknowledge that the abuse you endured was wrong.

The history, your parents' behavior, or their deeds cannot be changed. The only thing you can alter is you.

Respect your parents' restrictions.
Regardless of what you may believe, hope, or what they may say, accept that your abusive parents will never stop being abusive. In order to spare yourself future suffering, it is better that you accept this now.
If you are having problems accepting this, consider all the times they have promised to change or that you believed they would. Have they? Or did they end up disappointing you? Why would they suddenly change if they have continually failed you down?

Recognize that a parent who abuses their children is not capable of love, affection, or empathy. Stop holding onto the hope that they'll change. Do not hold out hope that they will ever change. I'm not advising you to forget or forgive, but rather to let go of the pain and resentment that have been weighing on you.

What does it means to accept your parents' limits ?

Accepting your parents for who they are entails accepting their flaws. This does not imply that you approve of their behavior, but rather that you acknowledge that they are flawed individuals.

Understanding them for who they are, with all their shortcomings and limitations, also means accepting that they were your parents and that you can't, even if you wanted to, replace them.

You will always look for someone or something to replace that parental hole in your life if you are unwilling to accept this truth.

You can look for a companion to take the position of the absent parent in your life. In relationships, you could develop codependency or overdependence. Additionally, you can feel entitled to them or depend on others to supply your demands.

Accepting your parent's restrictions at last

Once you've come to terms with your parents as they are, flaws and all,

You won't expect your parents to change or have any wishes or hopes for them.

You won't be looking for someone or something to take their place.

Instead of trying to have your wants met through relationships, you'll take care of yourself.

You won't view someone being there for you as something you owe them; instead, you'll regard it as an additional blessing. The portion of your life where you feel entitled to that parental nurturing will disappear once you have completely accepted the idea that your parents won't ever change and that that's just the way it is.

You must be prepared to mourn the loss. You must realize that you cannot go back and get it. And admit that you really can't make it happen with someone else.

You could still cherish the good times you had with your parents and wish you could relive those moments. However, be aware that in order to begin healing, you don't need to cease holding onto those memories.

You can recognize that your parents' actions make it challenging or even impossible for you to have a relationship with them while yet loving some aspects of them.

Reverse the cycle

You must begin healing from the abuse you experienced in order to guarantee that narcissism or emotional abuse won't be passed on to the next generation or even the next relationship in the future.

It's important to recognize that, despite how unpleasant it may be to hear, being an emotionally abused child may have left you with some of your abusive parent's characteristics. As they grow up, children learn from their role models.
It only makes sense that we would have taken up some of their habits and behaviors since that "role model" for us was our narcissistic parent. You can either manage or prevent it, though.

Additionally, whether you now have children or hope to in the future, the attitudes and actions you set an example for them are crucial. It is imperative that you avoid unintentionally instilling unfavorable attitudes and beliefs in your children. You can do better than your parents and stop the abusive cycle with your children, despite how difficult it may seem.

To feel better, we can deal with them differently by processing them and working with them. Reframing is the process of changing how you see a circumstance, person, relationship, or issue from an alternative angle.

We are all raised with scars. We are now who we are because of them. Try not to allow your scars, nonetheless, define who you are. Try to find strength in your scars instead.

Consider the benefits that your experiences have provided, and cultivate a spirit of gratitude. Although it might be very challenging, it is achievable and a vital step in the healing process.

Taking courage from my scars, your experience ought to motivate you to strive to be a better spouse, father, and all-around human being. It inspires me to go above and beyond to make sure my spouse and siblings know how much they are loved. You should be motivated to improve as a result.
It ought to encourage you further.

Additionally, it ought to increase your empathy and compassion for other people.

Taking courage from your scars

Your experience provided you with insight that can help other people. You can help others by using your inner wisdom. It's possible that you have certain strategies in the back of your mind to handle particular challenges.

You may become more conscious of other people, your surroundings, and yourself as a result.

You might want to make an effort to improve yourself and perhaps go out of your way to be a better person than your abuser. Make sure you never mistreat your spouse or children, if possible, in the same manner as your parents did.

In the end, even though your trip was difficult and painful, it was also one of change, development, and resiliency.

Learn who you really are.

There is a person below all the pain and suffering you have experienced. Do not allow your history or experiences to define who you are.

A big part of healing is looking for your true self.

Try to break free from your habitual incorrect, unthinking responses to other people and your surroundings. Recognize that how you react to people and the world isn't a reflection of who you are; it's a result of how you were raised. You are not defined by it.

In the past, being authentic was viewed as selfish or improper. but no longer. The moment has come to think about and prioritize YOU.

Get away from the abuse's negative repercussions.

Think about your principles and convictions.

Determine your hobbies, passions, and interests.

Consider what you desire from life.Be yourself and do what you want to do.

Never allow another person to define your identity or dictate your feelings or desires. Accept and embrace who you are, what you feel, and what you want.

Transform your life

When you are being abused, you are always on high alert and ready to avoid the next threat. This frequently results in ongoing anxiety and even a diminished sense of the future.

You probably experienced traumatizing abuse that caused you to develop a fearful outlook on life. You probably lost the ability to fully enjoy life or to think beyond the present because you grew so focused on just getting by.

The ideal future doesn't have to involve being well-known and wealthy while sipping martinis in a hot tub. But the future might just be a pipe dream. You are free to lead the life you wish.
Try to put an end to your self-doubt and start feeling good about yourself. You are capable of...

Be in the company of individuals who actually appreciate and adore you.
Without considering what others may think, do what you want to do and live your life as you like.
Be liberated in a way that you were unable to be when living under your parents' thumb as a child.
Live your life in accordance with your own principles, values, and beliefs.
True to who you are and what you desire, live your life.

To dream and hope for the future, try not to be fearful. Make an effort to overcome your fear and pursue your goals. You have a right to be content.

How to recognize your own healing?
Healing takes a lifetime. It's challenging to let go of something you've known and gotten used to for a very long time.

Because your past shaped who you are today, it is impossible to change the past or the impact it had and still has on you. But in order to help yourself grow and continue to recover, it's crucial to accept the past and make an effort to draw power from your suffering.

It would require daily work to prevent old tendencies from making a comeback. But keep in mind the advantages because they make the work worthwhile.
Begin repeating affirmations to yourself.

You must begin speaking while gazing in the mirror and begin continuously confirming your own worth.

Why must you express these things repeatedly each day? Because you mentally assume that your parents' unhappiness is your fault and that you are a "bad" child when your parents are not present for you in an attentive and nurturing way. Additionally, when your mother abuses you emotionally, she most likely also conveyed similar lessons to you by overt remarks or inference (guilt trips, silent treatments, pouting, etc.)

You've been feeding yourself negative thoughts for your whole life, so they're ingrained in your head. You must first repair the harm with encouraging affirmations in order to heal. The idea is to develop a positive internal voice that supports you.

You need to reprogram your brain. Your brain needs regular, consistent, interpersonally correcting input. So that your brain may be educated to think differently, this needs to occur repeatedly.

Conclusion

In the end, I hope we can come to a happy conclusion. But regrettably, you should never undervalue the influence of the familiar.

You'll be drawn to your previous habits and ideas, which could make you turn back into the person you were before. It's okay when that occurs as long as you don't remain there. And of course, make every effort to be mindful of it. When you notice that you are reverting, make an effort to stop.

You'll probably be on a lifelong healing journey. But try not to let it discourage you since if you keep going, things will become better and have a big impact on your life and wellbeing.

There will be ups and downs in equal measure. And those ups will get bigger as long as you stay on this course. It will require a lot of work and .

www.ingramcontent.com/pod-product-compliance
Lightning Source LLC
LaVergne TN
LVHW050338160826
845677LV00014B/3671

* 9 7 9 8 8 4 8 7 0 8 0 8 0 *